Cyberspace Intrusion

briel

Fair
ns

Okoyo Gabriel

Cyberspace Intrusions as a Threat to the Right to Free and Fair Elections

An Analysis of U.S. 2016 Presidential Election and Kenya 2017 General Elections

LAP LAMBERT Academic Publishing

Imprint
Any brand names and product names mentioned in this book are subject to trademark, brand or patent protection and are trademarks or registered trademarks of their respective holders. The use of brand names, product names, common names, trade names, product descriptions etc. even without a particular marking in this work is in no way to be construed to mean that such names may be regarded as unrestricted in respect of trademark and brand protection legislation and could thus be used by anyone.

Cover image: www.ingimage.com

Publisher:
LAP LAMBERT Academic Publishing
is a trademark of
International Book Market Service Ltd., member of OmniScriptum Publishing Group
17 Meldrum Street, Beau Bassin 71504, Mauritius

Printed at: see last page
ISBN: 978-620-0-53204-6

ACKNOWLEDGEMENTS

I'm so grateful to God for being so merciful and faithful unto me.

I'm greatly indebted and I must express my deepest appreciation to my Family, Mr. G. Qeu's family and Church members with whose unfailing love, prayers and support this work has become a reality.

In my heart also are the special gratitude to the Kisii University fraternity, and most specifically my supervisor and the Dean School of Law, Dr. Fred Nyagaka whom despite his academic accolades provided a very friendly environment for consultation, guidance and training.

I know many treasured people are part and parcel this achievement. I may not mention all, but I say THANK YOU VERY MUCH.

Okoyo Gabriel.

TABLE OF CONTENTS

CHAPTER ONE

Introduction

Democracy has withstood the test of time. It remains the most effective and progressive system of governance in the world today. As propounded by America's President Abraham Lincoln, democracy is a government of the people, by the people and for the people to rule. In a democratic state, every person has the right to be part of the leadership of his country either directly or through democratically elected representatives. This basic democratic principle is enunciated in Article 21 of Universal Declaration of Human Rights (UDHR) provides that such elections shall be periodic, genuine, by universal and equal suffrage and shall be held by secret vote or by any equivalent free voting procedures (UDHR, 1948). Almost similar provision and emphasis is echoed in Article 25 of the International Covenant on Civil and Political Rights (ICCPR). What is being entrenched by the said legal provisions is the underlying theme that the free will of the people and their equal participation in public affairs should be guaranteed. All citizens be given equal rights to cast ballot and vie for elective posts. Elections should be free and fair (ICCPR, 1966).

Today, in realization of this right, there is a sweeping move by many nations to convince their citizens that unlike the traditional pen and paper, the use of technology is the secure, clear, and only path to the ideal democratic land of free and fair elections. However, this research argues that there is more than what meets the eye of hopeful voters when it comes to the use of technology during an electioneering period. The use of technology in any election should be keenly analysed. The technological field is very competitive, characterised by fast evolving technologies, sharp ideological differences, superiority battles and high demand for profit by innovators and vendors. The efficiency of technological safeguards to ensure fairness and accuracy in any election is therefore such an important matter that should not be left solely at the mercy, whim and caprice of software developers, operators, hackers, vendors or big technology firms.

By analysing Kenya's 2017 and the US' 2016 election technology conundrums this research is putting forth and advancing an argument that in modern elections, the process of election begins as early as the time of technology software and hardware development. A credible, free and fair election, therefore, must enjoy maximum security and fair scrutiny of technological infrastructure. Here, much attention should be given to election software and hardware; development, storage, procurement, transportation, deployment and evaluation stages.

1

It is the researcher's contention that considering the escalating concern on cyberspace security, and the role of media in elections, technology should neither be perceived nor trusted as a fix-it-all phenomenon at any stage. Instead, technology should be treated holistically with great care, caution, vigilance, and as matter demanding national and international cooperation of stakeholders before, during and after elections (Moynihan, 2004).

Background Information on U.S. 2016 and Kenya's 2017 Elections

In October, 2017 Kenya concluded one of the most protracted presidential election in her post-independence history. The election was the sixth since the reestablishment of multipartism in 1991. However, when viewed from a democratization perspective, the electoral technology conundrum around Kenya's 2007, 2013 and 2017 general elections reaffirms one telling fact: that regular election are not by themselves an assurance for feasible democracy. Democracy is more than what visible exercise during voting and vote counting exercises. As evidenced by developed democracies, a government of the people, by the people and for the people to rule must be anchored on firm constitutional, legislative, administrative and institutional framework. This, however, must still be backed by a genuine political goodwill that provides strong pillars to support and consolidate democratic gains (Owuor, 2013). Ongoya and Otieno (2012) argue that in Kenya it is the thirst to satisfy the need for a sustainable democracy that propelled the clamour for a new constitutional dispensation. Undoubtedly, the clamour saw a resounding promulgation of the new Constitution of Kenya on August 27th, 2010 (Ongoya & Otieno, 2012).

One of the sectors that was inevitably affected by promulgation of the 2010 Constitution of Kenya was the electoral sector. Article 88 of the 2010 Constitution established an Independent Electoral and Boundaries Commission (IEBC) and clothed it with sole responsibility of organizing and overseeing referenda and elections. In executing its constitutional mandate, IEBC in 2013 introduced an Integrated Elections Management System (IEMS) to be used in the general elections (RoGGKenya.org, 2017). Unfortunately, and to the disappointment of many Kenyan electorates, the deployment of IEMS in the 2013 general election was marked by unforeseen mass failure in technology.

Learning from their past mistake, Kenyans continued with their unrelenting agitation for electoral reforms which undoubtedly saw the 2017 general election being run under a complex system of electoral laws. These included amendments to the Elections Act, 2011 to introduce the Kenya Integrated Electoral Management System (KIEMS). This KIEMS was the modern technology that was proposed to be used in Biometric Voter Registration (BVR), Electronic

Voter Identification (EVID) and as a Result Transmission System (RTS) where results are sent simultaneously in the form short messages (SMS) from the grass-root polling stations to the Constituency Tallying Centres (CTC) and finally to the National Tallying Centre (NTC).

With the deployment of KIEMS, the number of registered voters in the country during the Kenya's 2017 general elections was recorded as 19, 646,673. This was a record number not only attributed to the proper civic education, but also to the heated political campaigns that trumpeted the need for numbers in the election. The 2017 campaigns saw a fierce campaign between the sons of Kenya's founding fathers, Mzee Jomo Kenyatta's son Uhuru Muigai Kenyattta and Jaramogi Oginga Odinga's son, Raila Amollo Odinga. The dust settled, and on 11th August 2017, the IEBC Chairperson in exercising his mandate under Article 138(10) of the Constitution as the Returning Officer of the Presidential election declared Uhuru Muigai Kenyatta, the winner of the election with 8,203,290 votes and Raila Amollo Odinga, as the runner's up with 6,762,224 votes (*Presidential Petition No. 1 of 2017*,eKLR).

From a face value, one would believe that the 2017 general election was well accomplished by technology offering a sort of end to end solution. However, this is not the case. There was uproar from opposition sect that the electoral technology system used was hacked into and therefore the results did not reflect the true position and free will of Kenyans. Arguing in court in Presidential Petition No. 1 of 2017, it was the contention of the petitioners that the Independent Electoral and Boundaries Commission (IEBC) conducted the 2017 election so badly that it failed to comply with the governing principles established under the 2010 Constitution and the Elections Act (No. 24 of 2011) (*Presidential Petition. No. 1 of 2017, eKLR*). In their submission, the petitioners picked several issues with the Results Transmission System (RTS). They highlighted cases of inconsistencies in the scanned form 34A, 34B and 34Cs and also in SMS relayed results from polling stations to the Constituency Tallying Centre (CTC) and the National Tallying Centre (NTC).

In its historic final orders in favour of the petitioners, the Supreme Court by a majority of four to two dissenting opinions made and issued a declaration that the Presidential Election as conducted on 8th August, 2017 was not carried out in harmony with the 2010 Constitution and the enabling laws rendering the results therefrom invalid, null and void. Technology had failed the country in another election once again!

In the American presidential election held on November 8, 2016 things were not any better. The election is described by both winners and losers as a political earthquake (Faris et al., 2017). The

Republican Party Presidential candidate, Donald Trump, lost the popular vote to Democratic Party candidate, Hillary Clinton, by more than 2.8 million votes. However, he won 30 states and the decisive Electoral College with 304 electoral votes against Clinton's 227. He became the 45th president of the United States(Beckwith, 2016).

The tumultuous, abrasive 2016 campaign defied established political norms (Beckwith, 2016). As a candidate, Trump was obviously the most populist political candidate in the modern history. He openly staged an anti-conventional and anti-media campaign. Trump unswervingly expressed positions on immigration, trade, and international alliances, among many other issues, that were outside traditional consensus. He expressed his ideas in plain and aggressive terms. Even though his opponents could have perceived Trump's ideology and the way in which he communicated them as alarming, his supporters, however, perceived them as refreshing, timely and candid. He was sharply opposed, rebutted and may be sometimes overlooked by his opponents in both the primary and the general election, and yet he tremendously prevailed contrary to conventional wisdom and expectation (Faris et al., 2017) .

Damian Radcliffe argues that Trump presidency is to some extent a reflection of the status and evolution of the media and tech industries[1]. In particular, the role played by both domestic and international media and technology industries is still under heavy scrutiny, with Facebook's role in the rise of fake news currently enjoying considerable coverage (Radcliffe, 2016). Reports that Russian intelligence agencies were responsible for hacking the Democratic National Committee (DNC), disseminating the materials to WikiLeaks, and encouraging or reporting "fake news" on social media blog posts and other publications swirled around the final months of the 2016 presidential campaign. A hacker calling itself Guccifer 2.0 took credit for the leaks, and WikiLeaks would not reveal its source (Albarazi, 2016). Over the rest of the summer and early fall of 2016, some cyber experts and private security firms publicly asserted that the DNC hack had been conducted by Russian intelligence operatives and that it was directly controlled by the Russian government.

The scope and directness of Russia's actions towards the United States in 2016 was therefore unprecedented. It featured leaks of information Russia stole through cyber espionage, overt Russian propaganda, and hacks into election infrastructure, all three of which were distinct but were done at the same time and complemented each other(Treverton& Chen, 2017). In January

---

[1] https://www.salon.com/2016/12/07/the-tech-industry-and-the-media-can-share-blame-for-creating-donald-trump_partner/

2017, U.S. intelligence community deduced in an unclassified report that in the 2016 U.S. presidential election, Russia's aims were to create and manage public opinion and to undermine public faith in the U.S. democratic process via a scheme that blends covert intelligence operations such as cyberspace intrusions with overt efforts by Russian government agencies and proxies.[2]

This paper, therefore, seeks to analyse and bring out more on the operations that took place at cyberspace environment during the two elections, including material facts and allegations that surround, the procurement, deployment, and use of technology in elections. Cyberspace environment, as will be analysed later in this research, is not subject to the sovereignty of single state or group of states. It is global and borderless, open to participation by all, offers enormous potential for anonymity of participants and has low barriers to entry. Cyberspace therefore is inherently vulnerable to cross-border intrusions (GCHQ and Cert-UK, 2015.).

Problem statement

Waves of cyberspace intrusions are increasing in number, sophistication, targets and severity, Multinational companies, states' departments, servers and databases have been hit. As seen, the 2016 U.S. Presidential election and the 2017 Kenya general election became preys of alleged cyberspace intrusions. The impact of cyberspace intrusions in the two countries under focus exemplifies a problem which runs deep virtually all elections over the world. It is a reality which is contrary to what is expected if technology were to be insulated and properly deployed. This new twist by perpetrators to target elections is designed to manipulate election results, promote discord and undermine public confidence in countries democracy. Attempts to manipulate elections of sovereign states in whichever way is a move not only threatening the right to genuine, free and fair elections as envisaged in Article 21 of the 1948 UDHR, but also an imminent danger to sustainable democracy and trust. Unfortunately, these are the foundational rocks upon which international peace and stability of nations is anchored.

We, twenty-first century humans have trusted technology with the difficult, critical and important tasks of our lives. It's therefore not strange to find technology largely present in important areas of governments, taking advantage of the significant benefits that we are now used to everywhere else (Mugica, 2015). However, states should face an inflection point when it comes to the technology's effect on daily life of a state and citizens. What has enriched global

---

[2]Background to 'Assessing Russian activities and intentions in recent U.S. elections': The analytic process and cyber incident attribution," U.S. Office of the Director of National Intelligence, January 7, 2017, https://www.dni.gov/files/ documents/ICA_2017_01.pdf.

economy and quality of life for the past several decades may start to hurt us more than help us, unless we confront the cyberspace security challenges.[3] The role of mainstream and social media in election and investigations or study of electronic elections technology software and hardware has not been taken serious for a long time but could be very vital at this hour in advancing and protecting digital democracy.

Justification

As highlighted earlier, Cyberspace has become very central in human life. It's the environment where serious business is conducted, secrets sealed, critical information kept and where new governments are currently formed. Kenya's 2017 general elections and America's 2016 presidential election are under investigation over alleged poll interference in numerous ways. For instance, a federal jury in the United States has charged 13 Russian nationals and three Russian companies as part of the investigation into the alleged election meddling (Al Jazeera News, 2018). Cyberspace is slowly becoming a 21st Century jungle where the fittest and strongest survive, and a place for power struggle. The unfair and risky moves at cyberspace should therefore be thwarted by extensive study and awareness and those seeking to sow the soft seeds of war, confusion, discord, and rancor be hindered. Unfortunately, the jurisprudence of cyberspace law is not well developed and is not developing fast enough to guard and promote human rights at cyberspace. Instead, the private space and national border demarcations are fast fading at cyberspace, hence, necessitating a positive input in the field of cyber security. This study seeks to fill the gap by identifying the eminent threat and prescribing possible solutions to the challenges of cyberspace operations and regulation.

Objectives

In a world that is leaning towards the use of technology in every aspect of life, including elections, it is important to understand whether or not technology is serving and will continue to serve humanity well to achieve the desired goal in elections. This study therefore seeks to underscore the following objectives:

i.   To assess whether there is nexus between cyberspace intrusions and the right to free and fair election.

ii.   To evaluate how the nexus between cyberspace intrusions and the right to free and fair election impact on election outcome democracy and free will.

---

[3]For the purposes of this Article, "cybersecurity" means the protection of "computers, networks, programs and data from unintended or unauthorized access, change or destruction."

iii.   To find out how cyberspace can be made legally more effective in safeguarding the integrity of ballot and the will of the people.

Significance

This study is important in many ways: for instance, it positively contributes to the ongoing global discourse on cyber security and cyberspace threats. The recommendations as set out herein are vital when considering domestic electoral technology reforms. Internationally, this research is forming part of international studies and analysis that could be used by international policy makers and subsequent researchers. This research also churns the need to promote and advocate for human rights through cyberspace vigilance, awareness and cyberspace- security studies in the institutions of higher learning. To the general public, information is brought out the fore in order to enhance public know-how on matters of cyberspace security and the right to free and fair elections, relevant information on international relations and state's responsibility on matters of cyberspace security shall also not exceptional to the discourse herein.

Scope

This research has used majorly the events of Kenya's 2017 general election and US 2016 presidential elections as its major tools of analysis. However, in entirety of its analysis and data collection, the study has also analyzed, compared and contrasted different states' practices, legislations, cases laws, policies and reports. Specific countries like United Kingdom, Estonia and Germany which have had relevant experience and discussions around election technology are of great value for purposes of comparative analysis. The research has also taken keen study on relevant international law regime, best practices and policies.

Research question

The research will try to answer the following questions:

What is the nexus between cyberspace and right to free and fair elections?

What is the role of cyberspace and human factor in electronic voting in democratic elections?

Methodology

This study is relying on secondary sources of information, it has used books, encyclopedias, conventions, treaties, statutes, cases, journals, newspaper articles, magazines, television broadcasts, webpage, national and international policy papers, research papers, reports, thesis, speeches and materials such audio or video recordings of reputable scholars in the fields of cyberspace and election laws. Not an exception is also the researcher's own experience as an adult Kenyan citizen and as a voter during the Kenya's 2017 general elections.

CHAPTER TWO

There is a heavy burden on democratic states to run a competitive, peaceful, free and fair electoral process. The pressure from citizens, politicians and international donors is so intense that Election Management Bodies (EMBs) are rapidly adopting technology in their endeavour to resolve some deeply rooted electoral glitches. As a trend, players in the electoral process are also comfortable with moves towards technology. Through the expanding Internet-based electoral process, the Election Management Bodies, politicians, electorates and governments are collectively but virtually migrating to cyberspace domain. Conventional electoral operations on land and air spaces incessantly become minimal.

With the advent of artificial intelligence, smartphones, super computers and hybrid technologies cyberspace is well populated and busy, with everyone everywhere. Technology appears to be self-contained, immediate, so infinite and unavoidable that many users are insensitive to the larger context within which it operates and is embedded (Shah, 2012). Given its architecture and engineering, cyberspace generally provides neither assurance for human rights protection, data security, integrity, nor reliable information transmission secured against intrusions and other attacks.

This chapter, therefore, will identify the nexus between cyberspace intrusion and the human right to free and fair election. This will be done by, first, finding the definition of cyberspace and the meaning of cyberspace intrusion. Later, it shall find what really the words free and fair mean in the perspective of international human right. Finally, apart from general connection that would emerge in the course of writing, the research will lay out on its own sections the nexus between cyberspace intrusion and the right to free and fair elections.

The Meaning of Cyberspace

Books, films, and television programs of the 1980s paved a clear path for imagination, speculation, hope, and hype that has seen prominent inventions and developments in the field of Information Communication and Technology (ICT) (Zuley, James, & Cordell, 2003). For example, this term 'cyberspace' was coined in the 1984 novel *'Neuromancer'* by William Gibson, (Gibson, 1984). Cyberspace in Gibson's story was a science fiction when he wrote of it. Gibson employed the word to depict a "*mass consensual hallucination,*" a computer-made virtual reality where characters interacted heavily in computer- mediated environment (Bronk, 2016). Etymologically, cyberspace is a compound word and the origin of the initial term 'cyber' derives from the Greek term *kybernetes*, which means pilot, governor, or ruler[4]. The root word 'cyber' is also connected to '*cyborg*', a term that designates a human-machine amalgamation brought about by connecting the human body in advanced high-tech devices (Fourkas, 1999).

As a description of virtual space, cyberspace was conceived by William Gibson, in his novel as a three-dimensional 'data- scape' inside the global matrix of computer networks where disembodied users interact with clusters and constellations of data. He said;

> "… consensual hallucination experienced daily by billions of legitimate operators, in every nation, by children being taught mathematical concepts … A graphical representation of data abstracted from banks of every computer in the human system. Lines of light ranged in the non-space of the mind, clusters, and constellations of data. Like city lights, receding"(Gibson, 1984).

Ever since its conception in 1984, the fictitious '*cyberspace*' has been natured to reality with great expertise, care and services. Today, cyberspace exits as a reality with human. In appreciating its presence and existence, in 2003, US under the administration president Bush described cyberspace as the nervous system of critical national infrastructures and the control system of the country compromising hundreds of thousands of interconnected computers, servers, routers, switches and fibre optic cables that make the critical infrastructure work.

As years advanced, the U.S government agencies continued to study and analyse this virtual space that came from a fictitious novel. In 2009, the U.S government improved their definition. Now they described cyberspace as;

> "Global domain within the information environment consisting of the interdependent network of information technology infrastructures, including the internet, telecommunication network, computer systems, and embedded processors and controllers."[5]

(Eichensehr, 2015) maintains that governments and nongovernmental organizations have set out much similar definitions. For example, Germany defines cyberspace as;

---

[4] https://saavanahbourke.wordpress.com/2017/07/25/cyberspace/
[5] WHITE HOUSE, CYBERSPACE POLICY REVIEW 1 (2009), available at http://www.whitehouse.gov/assets/documents/Cyberspace Policy Review final.pdf (noting that this definition is included in National Security Presidential Directive 54 and Homeland Security Presidential Directive 23)

"the virtual space of all IT systems linked at data level on a global scale," and further explains that "[t]he basis for cyberspace is the Internet as a universal and publicly accessible connection and transport network which can be complemented and further expanded by any number of additional data networks," although "IT systems in an isolated virtual space are not part of cyberspace.''[6]

Kenya defines cyberspace as;

"The notional environment in which communication over computer networks occurs."[7]

While the United Kingdom describe it as;

"..an interactive domain made up of digital networks that is used to store, modify and communicate information," and notes that it "includes the internet, but also the other information systems that support our businesses, infrastructure and services.,"[8]

The International Organization for Standardization (ISO) gives their standard definition as;

"Complex environment resulting from the interaction of people, software and services on the Internet by means of technology devices and networks connected to it, which does not exist in any physical form."[9]

It's evident from the definitions that Cyberspace is a contemporary term in the field of ICT. There is no universally accepted definition despite the many attempts to define it. Different other states, organizations and individuals could be working around the clock to fashion a precise, flexible and universally accepted definition. However, from a backdrop of the existing attempts, the key embodiment of cyberspace can be deduced. Cyberspace can be described as having at least three layers: the technical, which is concerned with the technological infrastructure of cyberspace; the geographical, thus the topology of ICTs networks formed by the location of their nodes and hubs; and third is the social layer, which is concerned with the spatial organisation of people using the ICTs networks (Fourkas, 1999).

---

[6]FED.MINISTRY OF THE INTERIOR, CYBER SECURITY STRATEGY FOR GERMANY 14 (2011), available at http://www.cio.bund.de/SharedDocs/Publikationen/DE/Strategische-Themen/css_engl download.pdf?_blob=publicationFile.
[7]GovT OF KENYA, CYBERSECURITY STRATEGY 12 (2014), available at http://www.icta.go.ke/wp-content/uploads/2014/03/GOK-national-cybersecurity-strategy.pdf.
[8] U.K. CABINET OFFICE, THE UK CYBER SECURITY STRATEGY: PROTECTING AND PROMOTING THE UK IN A DIGITAL WORLD 11 (2011), available at https://www.gov.uk/government/publications/cyber-security-strategy.
[9] See ISO/IEC, Standing Document 6 (SD6): Glossary of IT Security Terminology (Oct. 16, 2014), http://www.jtc 1 sc27.din.de/cmd? Level=tpl-bereich&menuid= 64540&languageid= en&cmsare aid-64540.

With the foregoing, this research adopts and fully associates itself with the definition of cyberspace as presented by the government of United Kingdom. The UK identifies cyberspace as an interactive domain made up of digital networks that is used to store, modify and communicate information. And that it includes the internet, but also other information systems that support our businesses, infrastructure and services. Common among the definitions is also the view and acknowledgement of cyberspace as complex domain with unclear borders.

John Perry Barlow, a cyber-libertarian envisioned cyberspace as a free, non-hierarchical and borderless network of ideas and relations, where equality and justice could reign without governments exercising sovereignty over people's virtual lives. A civilisation of the mind in which information could flow without regulation or censorship. In his book *"Declaration of Independence of Cyberspace"* in 1996 Barlow proclaimed;

> "Governments of the Industrial World, you weary giants of flesh and steel, I come from Cyberspace, the new home of Mind. On behalf of the future, I ask you of the past to leave us alone. You are not welcome among us. You have no sovereignty where we gather..., cyberspace does not lie within your borders. Do not think that you can build it, as though it were a public construction project. You cannot. It is an act of nature and it grows itself through our collective actions" (Barlow, 1996). [10]

Barlow's written declaration was also one of the first representations of cyberspace as a political notion: it was to become a democratic space in which neither corporations nor governments could limit people's exercise of freedom. Effectively, the availability and free access of information and communication across the global Internet was meant to be an alternative to the traditional system of power held by states and private entities(Barlow, 1996). This view reflects the traditional understanding of cyberspace during the early days of its development. It was the conventional wisdom held by many that governments should stay of out of regulating cyberspace (Kalir & Maxwell, 2002). However, this traditional notion has since become obsolete. In a modern world where technology has become the central theme, currently there is an infringing technological arms race between those who seek to expand control and those who seek to minimize or escape it. Hence, data security and integrity is an overriding conceptual problem for all actors alike. Unless it is conceived of as an inter- national space, cyberspace takes all of the traditional principles of human rights protection and reduces them to absurdity (Menthe, 1998).

---

[10]https://www.eff.org/cyberspace-independence

Cyberspace Intrusion Explained

Intrusion in the context of cyberspace is; a violation of established borders, laws or rules as to data access in an information system where the violation may pertain to reading, modifying or corrupting protected data. As mentioned earlier, cyberspace is an interactive domain made up of digital networks that is used to store, modify and communicate information. It includes the internet and other information systems that support our businesses, infrastructure and services. From these constituent elements of cyberspace, it evident that almost all technologies embedded with an information system operate in this virtual space in one way or another. Cyberspace is the infrastructure of the modern world and the complexity of experience depends solely on the complexity of the technology (Shah, 2012).

As opposed to the land, air and sea, cyberspace is geographically limitless, has a great disrespect for jurisdictional boundaries, located in no particular location, its available to anyone anywhere in the world, and offers enormous potential for anonymity to its members. Traditional hierarchical power relations or concepts such as territorial sovereignty do not function in regards to cyber environment according to the same logic as in the physical world. At cyberspace people enjoy greater universal freedom. Users of digital technologies operate at cyberspace integrally in their daily functioning. Both state and non-state actors turn towards this digital space for their needs to communicate, interact, network, innovate and create new forms of expressions (Shah, 2012). Not exceptions are the Children who increasingly engage in internet games within cyberspace. While commenting about it, the former President of the United States, Mr Barack Obama stated;

> "It's long been said that the revolutions in communications and information technology have given birth to a virtual world. But make no mistake: This world -- cyberspace -- is a world that we depend on every single day. It's our hardware and our software, our desktops and laptops and cell phones and Blackberries that have become woven into every aspect of our lives..."

Cyberspace is real, and human beings, robots and other artificially intelligent machines are spending an increasing amount of time in the domain. All these players have diverse objectives, but via unique Internet tools they interact randomly in the virtual space. This interaction has led to spontaneous emergence of new threats that instigate a sense of fear and a need for counter measures. Gabriella Blum has noted that cyberspace is a world of distributed threats, easily available weapons, and of universal vulnerability (Carlin P. John, 2016). Hackers intrude into

12

different cyberspaces and employ diverse types of attacks ranging from; Service Disruption, Data Exfiltration, Bad Data Injection and Advanced Persistent Threat (APT) hacking computers is now a vehicle for spying, theft, expressing disobedience, exerting influence, manipulation and even perpetrating covert actions (Bronk, 2016).

Human being should seriously consider the fate of their rights at the digital environment. The days when cyberspace could be downplayed as a trivial issue in international security have passed. In recent years, the United States and other countries, including the United Kingdom, Israel, and Iran, have declared cyberspace as a "war domain" in the military context, like land, sea, air, and space (Eichensehr, 2015). The North Atlantic Treaty Organisation (NATO) declared at its July 2016 Summit in Warsaw, that the Alliance now considers cyberspace as a fifth operational domain . This essentially took NATO from the protection of the internal network (information assurance) to the cyber defence of every military activity (mission assurance) (Shea, 2016). Similarly, China's "Electronic Warfare strategy" have declared that electronic warfare is a vital fourth dimension to combat and should be considered equally with traditional ground, sea, and air forces.

As earlier mentioned, the relatively stringent rules, security and turf lines within the physical world are not replicated in the virtual realm. Increasing waves of severe and sophisticated cyberspace intrusions into public and private infrastructures render the traditional concepts of Sovereignty, Democracy and International Human Rights, within cyberspace much of antiquates. Cross-border cyberspace intrusions have resulted to loss of billions of dollars. The attack, dubbed "NotPetya," quickly spread worldwide, causing billions of dollars in damage across Europe, Asia, and the Americas[11]. Operators of critical system infrastructures like Electoral Management Bodies (EMBs) continue to worry of attacks against their machines and processes. Cyberspace, once a marvel, is now very much a mess (Bronk, 2016).

(Kostopoulos, 2018) maintains that the fundamental characteristics of a secure information system are its integrity, its availability, and its confidentiality. Cyberspace intrusions therefore targets majorly to undermine the confidentiality, integrity, or availability of a computer, or information resident on it. Intrusion can be perpetrated by hackers. These could be natural persons or artificially intelligent machines advancing an institutional, state or individual interest. The move is always against information systems with the intentions of data exfiltration, device

---

[11]See, Statement from the Press Secretary Issued on: February 15, 2018.
https://www.whitehouse.gov/briefings-statements/statement-press-secretary-25/

compromise, service disruption, bad data injection or advanced persistent threat (Miao Lu & Jason Reeves, 2014).

The information systems are not devoid of a defence mechanism, though. They are defended by dedicated traffic analysis systems which are designed to detect and hopefully block intrusions. Such systems, made of hardware and/ or software, are referred to as Intrusion Detection and Prevention Systems (IDPS). Depending on the particular application, a system may be an IDS, that is, only Intrusion Detection System with no prevention capabilities, or may be an IDPS, sometimes still referred to as IDS, that has both capabilities, detection as well as prevention. IDPSs implement rules established by the security administrator applicable to protecting access or entry points. Based on these rules, the IDPS passes, blocks, delays, or diverts data traffic (Kostopoulos, 2018). It is, however, the porosity and in effectiveness of this defence mechanism that puts the treasures in an information system in great jeopardy.

In order to establish and understand the nexus between cyberspace intrusions and the right to free and fair elections, the research will proceed to look at meaning and the constituent elements that make an election free and fair. It's building upon this foundation that we can appreciate the role of technology and cyberspace in an electoral process.

The Right to Free and Fair Election

Elections are a defining characteristic of democracy, and thus form an integral part of the democratization process (Ndulo & Lulo, 2010). If the average citizen, political parties and candidates do not perceive elections as free and fair, elections can stoke and foment conflict, which can lead to instability of a country with attendant economic breakdown(Maraga, n.d.) Substantially free and fair elections remain as the pillar that holds a constitutional democratic state together.

The Meaning of "Free and fair election"

according Universal Declaration of Human Rights (UDHR), the International Covenant for Civil and Political Rights (ICCPR) and many regional instruments, every- one has the right and must be provided with the opportunity to participate in the government and public affairs of his or her country, without any discrimination prohibited by international human rights principles and without any unreasonable restrictions. This right can be exercised directly, by participating in referenda, standing for elected office and by other means, or can be exercised through freely chosen representatives. The will of the people of a country is the basis for the authority of government, and that will must be determined through genuine periodic elections, which guarantee the right and opportunity to vote freely and to be elected fairly through universal and equal suffrage by secret balloting or equivalent free voting procedures, the results of which are accurately counted, announced and respected (European Union, 2016).

Article 25 of the ICCPR does not mention the phrase free and fair directly. However, it should be noted that the Articles of ICCPR are skeletons which are fleshed out by detailed UN General Comments. Consequently, the implications of the textual meaning of the provisions of Article 25 of ICCPR have been unpacked by the United Nations Human Rights Committee in its General Comment 25 as being:

On 26 March 1994, the Inter-Parliamentary Council unanimously adopted the Declaration on Criteria for Free and Fair Elections at its 154th Session Paris – France. The declaration provides among other things, that 'in any State the authority of the government can only derive from the will of the people as expressed in genuine, free and fair elections held at regular intervals on the basis of universal, equal and secret suffrage'. The Declaration was among the central and early attempts to set out what was required by the concept of a free and fair election, considered from the perspective of international law and human rights, and in the light of the practice of States and international organizations.(Goodwin-Gill, 2006). Goodwin-Gill states further that authority of the criteria declared in 1994 has since been repeatedly confirmed. For instance; The UN General Assembly took note of the Declaration (in resolution 49/190, 23 December 1994), and the criteria have also been incorporated into the practice of international organizations (including the UN's Electoral Assistance Division, UNDP, and regional organizations, such as the OSCE, the Council of Europe and the Organization of African Unity/African Union).

Since the adoption of the Declaration on Criteria for Free and Fair Elections in 1994, the Inter-Parliamentary Union has continued to contribute to the work of the United Nations and regional organizations, as well of its members, in the field of elections and democracy, and to keep its institutional focus on issues considered of paramount importance by the membership. In 1997, it adopted the Universal Declaration on Democracy, now frequently cited by other international organizations and State and non-State actors; and in 1998 it published Codes of Conduct for Elections, including a draft model code which addressed a number of factors relevant to the conduct of free and fair elections.(Goodwin-Gill, 2006)

According to Inter-Parliamentary Union, 2006, the requisite constituent elements for a free and fair election which informs international best practice are divided into the following ten broad categories: (i) Electoral law and system; (ii) Constituency delimitation; (iii) Election

15

management; (iv) The right to vote; (iv) Voter registration; (vi) Civic education and voter information; (vii) Candidates, political parties and political organization, including funding; (viii) Electoral campaigns, including protection and respect for fundamental human rights, political meetings, media access and coverage; (ix) Balloting, monitoring and results; and (x) Complaints and dispute resolution (Goodwin-Gill, 2006).

The Nexus Between Cyberspace Intrusions and the Right to Free and Fair Elections.

Digital technologies and the internet have affected how elections are conducted. Although reliance on computers and communication networks for elections has garnered some attention, election's cyberspace-security has not been politically prominent within democracies. (Fidler, 2017)

Cyberspace election intrusion shares some traits with other commonly known cyber-attacks. However, it is distinct in one substantial way; unlike most cyber-attacks, cyberspace election intrusion constitutes not only hacking, but also information campaigns. The special complexity of electoral process creates for cyberspace intruders a special nature of the target, requiring a special nature of an attack aimed at causing specific pre-designed damages. This could directly target citizens or state owned machines. Again, the propensity of other states involvement makes cyberspace election intrusions much complex than other forms of cyber-attacks. This is because when states are actors, the attack becomes difficult to identify, quantify, control, and remedy. These attacks, more often than not lack appropriate remedy, either within the domestic law or under international law regime.

The intrusive piece could be data designed to affect an electoral Information system, or propaganda released to make a sovereign's citizens think, act or vote in a certain way, thus impair independence of mind and any decision therefrom.

In order to map a nexus between cyberspace intrusion and the right to free and fair elections, I shall advance this research by first identifying the laws that introduced election technology in U.S and Kenya. Later, I shall plot the nexus between cyberspace intrusion and the right to free and fair elections by using the aforementioned constituent elements of free and fair elections as the major beacons.

The U.S., Help America Vote Act (HAVA), 2002

The legislation was borne out of the 2000 Presidential election controversy, which revealed the grave limitations of punch card voting and the need for investment in more modern and reliable voting systems. Congress passed the Help America Vote Act (HAVA), authorizing the allocation of $3 billion to states (based on voter populations), to fund the purchase of new voting technology.[12] The HAVA also created the Election Assistance Commission (EAC), a federal body tasked with providing guidance on voting technology standards and administering the HAVA funds (Hitt et al., 2016).

The Kenya Elections Act, 2011

The legal framework for Kenya's electoral system is contained in Articles 81 and 86 of the Constitution. In addition, Sections 39 (1) (C) and Section 44 (4), (5) and (7) of the Elections Act as amended in 2016 make provision for technology in Kenya's electoral law. Further, Section 44 (A) of the Election Act as amended in 2017 underpins the regime for election technology law. Other provisions of the Election Act provide the regulatory framework for the conduct of elections (Otieno-Odek, n.d.).

Cyberspace Intrusion and Election Management (Voter registration, balloting, monitoring and results

There is growing attempts by governments worldwide to run a smooth, peaceful and transparent electoral process. Many reforms to the process of election administration are apparently in the Election Management Bodies (EMBs) dedicated to manage the election process. Such bodies have assumed responsibility for a number of key electoral functions including; election technology implementation, determining who is eligible to vote, managing the nominations of parties and/or candidates, conducting the polling, counting the votes, and tabulating the results (Carter & Farrell, 2009).

The problem is that, for many Election Management Bodies, efficiency[13] has become an overriding value that must be pursued regardless of cost. Theologian Jacques Ellul observed that "technology has become...the defining force of a new social order in which efficiency is no longer an option but a necessity imposed on all human activity." Technology which was originally a skill or craft, a means by which to create a result or product has become an end in itself, and "the multiplicity of means is reduced to one: the most efficient." This idolatry of efficiency has led to a number of abuses in election management, ranging from gerrymandering

---

[12] See, "Election Costs: What States Pay," National Council of State Legislatures, June 16, 2016, http://www.ncsl.org/research/elections-and-campaigns/election-costs.aspx.

[13] Here efficiency means the extent to which time is used for the intended task.

of electoral delimitations to blind trust in voting systems that are so insecure and cannot be properly audited (Yard, 2010).

To begin with, a first category of election cyberspace intrusion is physical destruction of votes or voter equipment. A cyber-attack could exploit vulnerabilities in the voting systems to cause them to either suffer from physical damage, or else be out of use either through a malware infection of a denial of service attack.

A physical damage propagated by another state would make it easier to argue that the laws of war are applicable to this form of cyber interference. Experts have commented that this form of attack is possible. For instance in U.S due its out-of-date voting infrastructure across the nation. In the U.S. election system, the major subsystems of voter registration, election preparation, ballot casting, vote casting, and vote reporting each are vulnerable to this type of attack.[14] Most U.S. voting machines run Windows XP (for which security patches have been non-existent for at least three years). Researchers have noted that they are susceptible to malware or a denial of service attack("The Law of Cyber Interference in Elections," 2016)[15].

In Kenya Election Management Bodies have often been at the receiving end of attacks, criticism and blames for election technology mismanagement and failures. Election Management and Administration was at the core of the failure that was noted in the Disputed 2007 elections and constituted the main trigger for Kenya 2008 post-election violence. This was manifested by the scathing indictment by the Kriegler Commission on the then Electoral Commission of Kenya (ECK) (Owuor, 2013).

Cyberspace Intrusion, Civic Education and Voter Information
Technology and the Internet play an important role as a source of information for citizens and as a campaign tool for office seekers. They provide numerous benefits including: increased access to political information, ability to email/sms/social media pixel to target potential voters for money and vote, and ability to engage in online interactive political dialogue. During the Kenya 2017 election campaign period, President Uhuru Kenyatta and his opponent Raila Odinga frequently engaged their supporters via Facebook posts, video chats and twitter messages.

---

[14] https://www.washingtonpost.com/news/monkey- cage/wp/2016/11/07/a-cyberattack-could-disrupt-tuesdays-u-s-elections-but-wouldnt-change-the- results/?utm_term=.4ce5919a6ea1
[15] Brian Barrett, America's Electronic Voting Machines are Scarily Easy Targets, Wired (Aug. 2, 2016), https://www.wired.com/2016/08/americas-voting-machines-arent-ready-election/.

Cyberspace intrusion, however, is becoming a source of new threats to voter information. As seen during the U.S 2016 presidential election campaigns, 'Computational propaganda' is a serious cyberspace threat to voter information. This is "the use of algorithms, automation, and human curation (robots) to purposefully distribute misleading information over social media networks" (Polyakova & Boyer, 2018a). Voter Information in relation to election preparedness and campaigns should be of particular concern in the digital age. The twitter robots can quickly spread information to susceptible voters. It is important to note that sites such as Facebook, Google, and Twitter do not currently filter or flag fake news; they lack content editors, though they have begun to publically discuss the issue.

In the U.S 2016 presidential election, Russia-linked social media accounts on Twitter and Facebook were particularly adept at coupling automation with human curation. Robots were used to disseminate and spread counter Western narratives[16]. In their venture to control information and perception, Russia-linked actors often amplify divisive social issues. In Europe, those issues tend to focus on national sovereignty and immigration, Islam, terrorism, and the EU as a globalist, elitist body. In the United States, Russia's disinformation machine focused on racial tensions, criminal justice policy, immigration from Latin American and Muslim-majority countries, and class divisions. (Polyakova & Boyer, 2018a). The spread of fake news creates what Bruno Kahl, head of Germany's foreign intelligence service, calls "political uncertainty." Dissemination of news has the potential to disrupt elections, cause voters to doubt the democratic nature of outcomes, or cause voters to change their votes entirely.[17]

Cyberspace Intrusion and Political Parties

Cyberspace intrusion against democratic elections could also include operations against candidates and political parties. Democracies should not allow real or perceived cyber threats to election systems undermine the role voting plays in democratic sovereignty and to individual liberty (Fidler, 2017). Benjamin Reilly describes political parties as "the key agents of political articulation, aggregation and representation," making them "the institutions which impact most directly on the extent to which social cleavages are translated into national politics. However,

---

[16] See; Algorithms, bots, and political communication in the US 2016 election: The challenge of automated political communication for election law and administration - https://www.tandfonline.com/doi/full/10.1080/19331681.2018.1448735

[17]See, Kathy Gilsinan and KrishandevCalamur, Did Putin Direct Russian Hacking? And Other Big Questions, The Atlantic (Jan. 6, 2017), https://www.theatlantic.com/international/archive/2017/01/russian-hacking- trump/510689/.

most political parties are often polarised by conflicting political- ambition of top party leaders. This makes parties weak and vulnerable to malicious intrusion from insiders or external hackers. In Kenya, political parties are structurally weak, and they typically lack orientation, focus or ideology. Often the parties are based on individuals or ethnic divides rather than a clear program, leaving voters with the unappealing choice between the "devil they know" and the possibly-worse "unknown." (Ndulo & Lulo, 2010)

Political parties can be perpetrators or victims of cyberspace intrusion. In Kenya, during and after the 2017 general elections, National Super Alliance (NASA) persistently claimed that contrary to the results declared by IEBC, they had the 'genuine and true' results that they got 'unofficially' from the IEBC servers. NASA proceeded even to publicly publish the results claiming they were the genuine figures contained in the IEBC servers and that Kenyans should believe them. The question that was repeatedly asked and which NASA officials kept on brushing away is 'how NASA's IT experts or their 'protected whistle-blowers' got the data? IEBC brushed off NASA'S data and considered them as mere political rhetoric. This research argues that such statements, confessions or allegations of unofficially acquiring data from an Electoral Body should be treated seriously. This is because, they are classical indicators of either failed or successful attempts of data exfiltration, service disruption or bad data injection at worst.

During the U.S 2016 presidential election campaigns, the Democrats Party became a victim of cyberspace intrusion. U.S. intelligence agencies and private cyber security firms identified two groups with ties to Russian intelligence that were involved in the hacking of the Democratic National Committee (DNC). The hack led to a series of politically harmful emails being publicly leaked ahead of the U.S. presidential election.[18]

Cyberspace Intrusion and Candidates

Cyberspace Intrusion against election candidates is an emerging trend mostly in advanced democracies. The intrusion is intended to upload or download information, pictures or videos specially assorted to harm her a candidate's electability and potential. During the 2016 U.S presidential campaigns, Hillary Clinton claimed that Donald Trump personally invited the Russians to hack into her email servers. Trump is quoted by her to have allegedly said: "Russia, if you're listening, I hope you're able to find the 30,000 emails that are missing," he said, adding "[b]y the way, they hacked—they probably have her 33,000 e-mails. I hope they do. They

---

[18] Roland Oliphant, "Who are Russia's cyber-warriors and what should the West do about them?" The Telegraph, December 16, 2016, http://www.telegraph.co.uk/news/2016/12/16/russias-cyber-warriors-should-west-do/.

probably have her 33,000 e-mails that she lost and deleted because you'd see some beauties there. So let's see"[19]. Regardless of where the truth lies, the fact remains that the email servers were hacked and the release of the emails had a far reaching consequences on Hillary Clinton presidential candidacy.

In Kenya, intrusions against candidate's personal information were not reported. However, In France, Emmanuel Macron is said to have been a target of disinformation by Russia-linked cyberspace operations in 2017. It is alleged that the Russian intelligence agents created fake and deceptive Facebook accounts for purposes of spying on then-candidate Emanuel Macron. Troves of emails were hacked from Macron campaign officials. The stolen emails were then posted publicly just two days to the elections, during the period when media were no longer allowed to report on the elections in accordance with French law, the Twitter campaign #MacronLeaks reached 47,000 tweets in just 3.5 hours after the initial tweet.[20]

Cyberspace, however, continues to offer more and more weapons and the battlefield to attack candidates in future. For instance, fuelled by artificial intelligence, digital impersonation is on the rise. Machine-learning algorithms (often neural networks) combined with facial-mapping software enable the cheap and easy fabrication of content that hijacks one's identity—voice, face, body. Deep fake technology inserts individuals' faces into videos without their permission. The result is "believable videos of people doing and saying things they never did." not surprisingly, this concept has been quickly leveraged to sleazy ends. The latest craze is fake sex videos featuring celebrities like Gal Gadot and Emma Watson.[21] It can be predicted with certainty that this is another dangerous weapon for onslaught of democracy at cyberspace.

Cyberspace Intrusion, Electoral Campaigns, Media Access, and Coverage
During the 2016 U.S. presidential election period, fears that foreign actors could exploit cyber technologies in an attempt to manipulate data and transmission of results to influence election outcomes multiplied among policymakers and the general public. Russian information operations and disinformation on social media coupled with Hillary ad DNC hacks justified these fear.

---

[19] Andy Sherman, Hillary Clinton Claims Donald Trump Invited Russian President Vladimir Putin to Hack Americans, Politifact (Sept. 26, 2016), http://www.politifact.com/truth-o-meter/statements/2016/sep/26/hillary-clinton/hillary-clinton-claims-donald-trump-invited-russia/.

[20]Hashtag campaign: #MacronLeaks," DRFLab, May 5, 2017, https://medium.com/dfrlab/hashtag-campaign-macronleaks- 4a3fb870c4e8

[21] See blog post on democracy and privacy;https://lawfareblog.com/deep-fakes-looming-crisis-national-security-democracy-and-privacy

Election cyberspace security therefore called for preparations and due diligence against any possible foreign interference with the election's integrity. Parallel concerns and worries have arisen with regards to other elections in France, Britain, and Germany. For the state of Netherlands, they ultimately opted to hand count ballots in election to put off any hacking thinking or attempt that would affect the election outcome.

On campaigns, media access and coverage, both candidates for political positions in U.S and Kenya have ascertained and embraced that the most effective way to make news or reach vast audience is to post a picture, statement or comment in a social media platform. This has since overturned the long dominance of TV stations as avenues for successful campaigns. (Bambara, Kapsis, Koonce, Ungar, & Webb, 2016).

Cyberspace Intrusion, Protection and Respect for Fundamental Human Rights

Traditionally, cyberspace threats have been associated with the right to privacy and freedom of speech. This research argues that elections cyberspace intrusions, however, now puts more rights in danger of grievous and irreparable violations. The 2017 Kenyan killing of the IEBC's Acting Director of ICT, Chris Msando just few weeks to elections could be a case in study. The death of Msando casted a grave pall over election preparations. As the official who oversaw the implementation of the integrated elections management system, which includes biometric voter identification and electronic results transmission, Msando played a critical role. His murder sparked serious fear about the security of the IEBC's systems and the potential for outside intervention in the data that feeds that system (Kura Yangu Sauti Yangu, 2017). In this paper, I consider Msando's murder as a violent and bloody attempt to intrude into a critical information system infrastructure. Whether or not Msando's death affected the election technology and the ultimate election process and result will be discussed at length in the next chapter of this research.

Cyberspace Intrusion, Complaints and Dispute Resolution

After the "hanging chad" controversy of the 2000 U.S. presidential election, the U.S. Congress enacted the Help America Vote Act of 2002 (HAVA). The adoption HAVA initiated the use electronic voting machines. Consequently the computer, information, and network security became coeval to electoral integrity (Fidler, 2017). While the electronic voting machines have not yet been subject to allegations of malicious activity, some state election infrastructure have experienced cyberspace intrusion. For instance, Illinois and Arizona voter registration databases are alleged to have been accessed by Russian hackers and over 200,000 voter registration data were exposed in these breaches. There are, however, no indications that the information in these records was altered and the intrusion cannot yet be definitively attributed to the Russian government (Shackelford et al., 2017). Cyberspace has brought many complaints; the biggest problem is that dispute resolution for cyberspace intrusions is so complex and quite demanding.

Kenya struggled with election management and dispute resolution for a long time till 2007. About 4months to the 2007 general elections, the Election Commission of Kenya (ECK) outsourced development of an integrated system. This system was designed to allow vote data entry at the constituency level, and transmit the same data directly by communication with headquarters via a wireless general packet radio service (GPRS) linking to a laptop computers in constituency headquarters (Yard, 2010). Technology was intended to solve some deeply rooted election disputes and complaints. However, this technology terribly failed creating a devastating impact of conflict, in particular the 2007–08 postelection violence.

Kenyan election dispute resolution is complex, involving multiple resolution bodies with, at times, overlapping jurisdiction and inconsistent deadlines. (The Carter Centre, 2018). During the presidential petition at the Supreme Court, the difficulty with which the court and the advocates approached technology issues was publicly manifested. Another challenge with cyberspace intrusion dispute resolution is faced while trying to solve international disputes. For instance, French digital-security company OT-Morpho, whose equipment was used in Kenya's presidential election, reiterated that its systems weren't tampered with to rig the outcome, calling the accusations an attempt to shift blame for a vote the nation's Supreme Court nullified. This is despite the fact that the Supreme Court order in regard to data access was partly complied with leaving the other parts for speculations whether the system was indeed tampered with necessitating the denial of full compliance with court order (Preiss, 2017).

Cyberspace Intrusion, Electoral Law and System
What is common in all cases is that the choice of a particular electoral system has a great consequence on the future political life of the country so adopting it. Electoral systems, once preferred, often remain constant as political stakes solidify around and react to the spurs presented by them. There are three major electoral systems; Plurality Systems (sometimes referred to as First Past The Post the (FPTP)); Proportional Representation Systems, and Mixed Systems. Both Kenya and U.S uses Plurality/Majority Systems. First Past The Post the (FPTP) is the modest form of this plurality/majority system. The system uses using single- member districts and candidate- focused voting (Reynolds, Reilly, Ellis, Cheibub, & Cox, 2008). A voter

is offered the names of the nominated candidates and he/she votes by electing one, and only one, of the candidates. The winner then becomes the candidate who wins most votes. In theory and as an elaboration thereto, the winner could be elected with two votes, if all other candidate only garnered a single vote each. Basically, the winner is the candidate who gains many votes than any other candidates, even if this is not an outright majority of valid votes casted.

To date, pure FPTP systems can be traced primarily in the UK and countries historically influenced by Britain. Together with the UK, the systems more often analysed includes the United States, Canada, and India. It's important to note that despite Kenya employing a FPTP system for other elective seats; it uses a Two-Round System (TRS) when it comes to presidential elections. A Two-Round System is a plurality/majority arrangement in which a second election is conducted if neither a candidate nor party garners a given number of votes in the first round of election, normally an absolute majority of 50per cent plus one.

Notwithstanding the electoral design, one thing remains very common and crucial, that in all systems every single vote is important and substantial in influencing the outcome of an election. Electoral management bodies must therefore be under profound scrutiny as politicians would seek to exploit any slightest flaw in a system.(Yard, 2010).

Conclusion

Inter-Parliamentary Union outlines the aforementioned fundamentals of a free and fair election (Goodwin-Gill, 2006). This chapter has just looked into the nexus between cyberspace intrusion and some of them. However, with the increased use of technology by both states and private citizens, all the elements listed are critically affected by technology. A proper analysis of the right to free and fair election must therefore shift to the conducts and operations at cyberspace. Election cyberspace intrusions have begun, but it's nowhere close to ending. As will be discussed in the next chapter, it therefore prudent to study the impact of this intrusion to the right to free and fair election in order to pave way for appropriate measures.

CHAPTER 3

This chapter will evaluate how the nexus established in the previous chapter, between cyberspace intrusion and the right to free and fair elections impact on elections outcome and peoples free will. For effective evaluation of the topic, the effect cyberspace intrusions in Kenya's 2017 electoral process is dissected into three major stages, that is: Pre-election intrusions, Intrusions during Voting, tallying and result transmission; and finally, Post-election intrusions. United

States being a more advanced democracy with a more stringent cyber-security, the intrusions were not grossly manifested in the three stages as the case in Kenya, hence, for the U.S. 2016 Presidential election, this research limit itself to the notorious pre-election or campaign period intrusions. It is on this foundation that we can easily analyze and appreciate the impact of cyberspace intrusions on democracy. This research will undoubtedly take this roadmap and begin by analyzing pre-election cyberspace intrusions in the U.S. 2016 Presidential election.

The Impact of Cyberspace Intrusions on Election Outcome and Free Will in the 2016 U.S Presidential Elections

In 2016, the US political arrangements and practises were done before a mass of international audience.In this age of overreliance on cyberspace operations digital trends are escalating and deepening. The internet has provided new opportunities for public participation in political debate, through platforms such as blogging, and social media. Websites such as YouTube permitted political groups to make statements with global reach For all these reasons, then, an understanding of the contemporary political process is inconceivable without an analysis of the media (Introduction & Communication, 2018).

In the 2016 US Presidential elections, conventional forms campaigns were employed; however, fierce ideological wars, liberation struggles and reputation deconstruction was highly fought out in the media, with global public opinion as the prize[22] this research argues that in America cyberspace intrusion was manifested in two forms; information theft and voter information. This paper will discuss these two forms as below.

Voter Information

The 2016 United States presidential election was covered by tens of thousands of separate media entities that together compose a complex media landscape(Faris et al., 2017). Voters received their political information and news from a diverse set of specialized sources, many of which are designed to serve mass audiences. One of the greatest players in this filed was facebook and twitter(Faris et al., 2017).

Hillary Clinton for example publicly declared her presidential bid by tweeting:

'I'm running for president. Everyday Americans need a champion, and I want to be that champion. – H' (tweet, 12 April 2015)[23].

---

[22] ibid
[23] https://twitter.com/hillaryclinton/status/587336319321407488?lang=en

25

Rather than calling a press conference and relying on the mainstream media to share her news, Clinton's campaign team resorted to Twitter and YouTube, via a YouTube video release titled 'Getting started', in which Hillary Clinton tells the world that she is 'getting ready to run for president'[24]. Likewise, social media provided Donald Trump with a platform to critique the main- stream media as biased and untrustworthy (Enli, 2017). However, the presidential candidates and the electorates were not the only senders and recipients of information on American cyberspace. Automated accounts run by twitter robots were part and parcel of the American political discussion and opinion shaping.

Twitter Bots

Bots are social media accounts that automate interaction with other users, particularly; political bots have been active on public policy issues, political crises, and elections. A growing number of political actors and governments worldwide than 4 percent of the re-tweets he received from Sept. 1 to Nov. 15, 2016. Hillary Clinton's account got less than 50,000 retweets by the Russian-linked automated accounts during the same period[25]. Even though this is a case still under investigations and study, one thing comes out clearly; that Bots can perform critical tasks like delivering news and information, or undertake malicious activities like spamming, harassment and hate speech. Whatever their uses, bots have now proved their capacity to rapidly deploy messages, replicate themselves, and pass as human users. During the 2016 U.S. electioneering period, bot accounts generated approximately 2.12 million automated, election-related tweets, which collectively received approximately 454.7 million impressions generated within the first seven days of posting(Twitter Inc., 2018).

Political bots tend to be developed and deployed in sensitive political moments when public opinion is polarized. An analysis of how bots were used during the Presidential debate by sampling the hashtags associated with the Presidential candidates or the @realDonaldTrump and @HillaryClinton account names revealed that; a reasonably consistent proportion of the traffic on these hashtags were posted by highly automated accounts. These accounts are often bots that see occasional human curation, or they are actively maintained by people who employ scheduling algorithms and other applications for automating social media communication(Kollanyi, Howard, & Woolley, 2016).

---

[24]https://www.youtube.com/watch?v=0uY7gLZDmn4

[25]https://www.bloomberg.com/news/articles/2018-01-26/twitter-says-russian-linked-bots-retweeted-trump-470-000-times

This information underscores the how Russian-linked bots intruded into America's cyberspace and sought to stir up discord during the 2016 U.S. presidential election. These undoubtedly took part in many sensitive political topics during electoral contest. For instance, Twitter Company states that;

> "During the relevant time period, @Wikileaks Tweets were Retweeted approximately 5.65 million times. Of these, about 196,836 or 3.48% retweets, were from Russian-linked automated accounts. The Tweets from @DCLeaks_ during this time period were Retweeted 6,774 times, of which 2.47% were from Russian-linked automated accounts. The Tweets from @GUCCIFER_2 during this time period were Retweeted approximately 24,000 times, of which 2.32% were from Russian-linked automated accounts.(Twitter Inc., 2018)"

Automated accounts have become weapons and means of controlling people, by going beyond amplifying follower lists to retweeting volumes of designed commentary. It must be taken serious that voter information runs to the core of democracy, to the hammock of a free and fair election. Twitter reports that some of the bots' accounts appear to have attempted to organize rallies and demonstrations, and several engaged in abusive behaviour and harassment(Twitter Inc., 2018).

This research argues that bots have proven their capability and shown their effectiveness in putting stuff into voters' feeds, and in amplifying messages.In U.S. 2016 Presidential election, the Russian bot army stirred-up division around such topics as white supremacist marches and police violence.

The predominant aim, during the election, analysts say, was to expand and exploit divisions, attacking the Americans' social fabric where it is most susceptible, along lines of race, gender, class and creed[26].

According to Tom McCarthy, the intruder pages included 'Secured Borders', an anti-immigrant account that grew to 133,000 followers; 'Texas Rebels', which parroted Lone Star state pride while criticizing Clinton; 'Being Patriotic', which criticized refugees while shielding the Confederate battle flag; 'LGBT United', which subtly espoused "traditional" family values; and 'Blacktivists', a faux satellite of the Black Lives Matter movement. Further, and according to Tom Russia-linked imposters had millions of interactions on Facebook with prospective voters

---

[26]https://www.theguardian.com/us-news/2017/oct/14/russia-us-politics-social-media-facebook

who believed they were interacting with fellow Americans. He argues, that these interactions may have reinforced the voters' political views or helped to mold them.[27].

According(Polyakova& Boyer, 2018b) Russia's current disinformation model is premised on the concept of a "fire-hose of falsehood", repetitive, fast paced, continuous, high-volume information attacks from a variety of sources. The aim being to muddle the notion of truth or objectivity, blur the line between fact and falsehood, and sowing confusion among publics.

Information Theft

On June 15, 2016 one day after the Democratic National Committee (DNC) cyber-attack became public, a hacker named Guccifer 2.0 thought to be in the forefront of Russian intelligence claimed credit for the breach and posted a cache of stolen documents. Guccifer bragged that he had given thousands more to WikiLeaks, the organization apparently ardent to radical transparency. WikiLeaks founder, Julian Assange, followed by promising to release emails related to Hillary Clinton. This surely came to pass. Hillary Clinton states that the publication of the stolen files from the DNC was a dramatic turn of events for several reasons; For starters, it exhibited that Russia was so interested in doing more than collecting intelligence on the American political cyberspace; it was enthusiastically trying to manipulate the election. Clinton claims that just as it had done a year earlier with the audio recording of ToriaNuland, Russia was so keen on 'weaponizing' the stolen information to the detriment democracy.(Clinton, 2017).

According to Hillary Clinton, the impact of the hacks was real and grievous on her candidacy. WikiLeaks published about twenty thousand stolen DNC emails on July 22, 2018. It highlighted some of messages that included unpleasant comments about Bernie Sanders, which in all likelihood was designed to set off a firestorm among Bernie's supporters, majority of whom were still indignant for having lost the primaries[28]. However, to Hillary's relief, nothing in the stolen emails remotely backed up the accusation that the democrat's primaries had been rigged. Nearly all of the offending messages were written in May, just few months after Hillary had gathered an overwhelming vote and delegate lead. But as a blow to Hillary's campaign, DNC chair Debbie Wasserman Schultz resigned two days later, and the opening of the convention was marred by loud boos and catcalls from Sanders supporters[29]. In her book, 'What Happened', Hillary states that;

> "As painful as it is to return to this maddening saga, it's now more important than ever to try to understand how this issue ballooned into an election-tipping controversy. A lot of people

---

[27] ibid
[28] Clinton, H. (2017). *What Happened*. New York: Simon & Schuster.
[29] ibid

still don't understand what it was all about; they just know it was bad. And I can't blame them: they were told that over and over again for a year and a half. For most of the general election campaign, the word email dominated all others when people were asked to name the first word that came to mind about me......throughout the 2016 campaign, I watched how lies insinuate themselves into people's brains if hammered often enough. Truth examination is powerless to pull it up." (Clinton, 2017).

Hillary says that her friend who made calls or knocked on doors for her would talk to people who confessed they couldn't vote for her because she had killed someone, sold drugs, and committed some number of unreported crimes, including how she handled her emails.

This research argues that the bots repeated the attacks so frequently that many voters took it as an article of faith that Hillary must have done something wrong[30]. As though in furry, Hillary declares THE Americans that;

> "What should be beyond doubt is that foreign interference in our elections is wrong, period. And the threat we face, from without and within, is bigger than one campaign, one party, or one election. The only way to heal our democracy and protect it for the future is to understand the threat and defeat it"[31].

This is an emerging episode, a matter that most scholars, security experts and political players still consider fresh and under scrutiny. As preamble to the investigation, a special counsel investigating Russian intervention in the 2016 presidential election indicted 12 Russian intelligence officers for hacking the Democratic National Committee and Hillary Clinton's campaign[32]. It is argued that the indictment was significant because it, for the first time, explicitly and publicly implicates the Russian government in the hacking effort, a central part of that country's apparent attempt to manipulate the outcome of the election.

The indictment itself offers a flurry of new details about that effort, including, perhaps most importantly, that the hackers tried to access Clinton's personal server on July 27, 2016 — the same day[33]

This research argues that the conundrum surrounding the U.S. 2016 elections is still under investigation and more is yet to come to light. The FBI and the Department of Homeland Security (DHS) had released a joint report detailing how federal investigators linked the Russian

---

[30] Clinton, H. (2017). *What Happened*. New York: Simon & Schuster.

[31] ibid

[32] https://www.nytimes.com/interactive/2018/07/13/us/politics/how-russia-hacked-the-2016-presidential-election.html

[33] https://www.washingtonpost.com/news/politics/wp/2018/07/13/timeline-how-russian-agents-allegedly-hacked-the-dnc-and-clintons-campaign/?noredirect=on&utm_term=.a774d23152f5

government to hacks of during the electioneering period. Though it does not mention either by name, the report makes clear reference to the hacks of the Democratic National Committee (DNC) and campaign chairman John Podesta. The report provides technical details in relation to tools and infrastructure employed by Russian hackers and military intelligence services to compromise and exploit networks. However, security experts say that the document provides little in the way of forensic evidence to confirm the government's attribution.

On April 20, 2018 the Democratic National Committee filed a lawsuit against the Russian government, the Trump campaign team and WikiLeaks. The case which was filed in the federal district court in Manhattan, alleges that chief Trump campaign officials connived with the Russian government and its military spy agency to ruin Democratic presidential nominee Hillary Clinton and aid Trump by hacking the computer networks of the Democratic Party and disseminating stolen materials found there. In the lawsuit, the complainants contend that Russia is not entitled to sovereign immunity in the case because the claims arise out of Russia's intrusion on to the DNC's private servers in an illegal endeavour to steal trade secrets and commit economic espionage. DNC is seeking millions of dollars in compensation to indemnify the damage it claims the party suffered from the hacks. The DNC argues that the cyber-attack undermined its ability to communicate with voters, collect donations and operate effectively as its employees faced personal harassment and, in some cases, death threats.[34]

The Impact of Cyberspace Intrusion on Election Outcome and Free will in Kenya 2017 General Elections

Following the 2007/2008 Kenya post-election violence the Government formed the Independent Review Commission (IREC), which has been commonly referred to as Kriegler Commission. The commission was to inquire into the events of the 2007 elections and the genesis of Kenya's worst violence. The Commission's focus, among other issues was drawn to the integrity of vote counting, tallying and declaration of presidential election results. In relation these, the commission made various recommendations as set forth in their report.

In an endeavor to avoid the repeat of 2007/2008 events, and by acting upon the Kriegler Commission recommendations, the process of integrating technology into the conduct of elections was instituted. This began with the use of Biometric Voter Registration (BVR)

---

[34]https://www.washingtonpost.com/politics/democratic-party-files-lawsuit-alleging-russia-the-trump-campaign-and-wikileaks-conspired-to-disrupt-the-2016-campaign/2018/04/20/befe8364-4418-11e8-8569-26fda6b404c7_story.html

equipment to register voters preceding the 2010 referendum. Later, in 2013 elections technology was again deployed for registration of voters, voter identification and results transmission. Unfortunately, that did not work very well in the 2013 general election and it became one of the major grounds raised in the 2013 presidential petition before the Supreme Court. Consequently, in 2016 a Joint Parliamentary Select Committee on matters relating to the bi-partisan Independent Electoral and Boundaries Commission (IEBC) was formed. The product was extensive amendments to Elections Act to explicitly provide for use of technology. Special dedication to technology was further made via Elections (Technology) Regulations 2017. All these, plus many other reforms were meant to streamline electoral process, entrench the will of the people and to make democracy harder hack.

The objective, however, cannot be said to have been achieved. In Presidential petition No.1 of 2017, the petitioner's successful complaint still as a matter of Kenya's tradition revolved around technology, vote tallying and transmission of results.

This research argues that such complaints can never end unless issues of cyberspace intrusions is properly analyzed and addressed. In an attempt to evaluate and show the impact of cyberspace intrusion on elections outcome and free will in, the research will make specific reference to Pre-election, Election Day, and Post-election occurrences that points towards successful intrusions and intrusion attempts. Critical analysis, however, will be given to the Supreme Court decision in the case of RailaOdinga& Another vs. IEBC& 2 others (*Presidential Petition No. 1 of 2017*)

Pre-election Intrusions in Kenya 2017 General Elections.

Pre-election intrusions in Kenya can be best analysed by looking at cyberspace vis-à-vis voter registration, voter information, campaigns, and IEBC's system and officials. As a trend, election rigging via cyberspace intrusions is becoming the norm. It's a multi-billion-dollar industry, pompous offers flow and contracts are sealed with those who produce 'right' outcome as per the client. For instance, in Kenya, Cambridge Analytica is said to have been paid $6 million to support the campaign of President Uhuru Kenyatta. This research argues that there are many more such contracts for despotic manipulation of voters' free will both locally and internationally. Companies and individuals seeking these tenders are constantly coming up with innovative ways to subvert democracy. (Forsyth, Liddle, Thomas, Moore, & Holland, 2018)

The strategy is always to; first, intrude into the cyberspace of the targeted state. This is done by either having agent(s) operating online while physically present within the jurisdiction of targeted state, or by being physically outside the targeted state, but virtually present and active

31

within its cyberspace via social media and malicious internet related operations. As stated earlier, these operations range from service meddling, data mining, introduction of foreign data. Hackers study the political and information topography within which they intend to operate. Depending on the motivation, their effect is then manifested through the spreading fake news, vicious attacks, memes, blogs, graphics, pictures, and videos all intended to bring down their client's opponents.

Another shocking pre-election occurrence was the mysterious murder of Mr.Chris Musando. Mr. Musando was the IEBC ICT manager. This research argues that the murder of Musando few days to election was neither an accident nor a matter bad coincidence. It was strategically designed. The murder should be attributed to nothing other than an extreme calculated move by cyberspace intruders. This was such a daring move by perpetrators of cyberspace. It is an evidence that those who seek to manipulate elections have since changed their target and strategy. The main target is now how to control the electoral cyberspace. The bloody land and air campaigns are diminishing and politicians no longer fight for microphones. Instead, the battle is taken online and each antagonising camp is seeking to monopolize and control social media, mainstream media, and more so the computer systems that are managed by the Electoral Management Bodies like IEBC.

Perpetrators of cyberspace intrusion can make any move so as to deliver their promise, manifest their capability and have their dues. This research argues that such perpetrators are often an organised group of sharp minds headed by intellectuals and IT gurus with outstanding academic accolades or experience. They will, therefore, do anything within the corpus of their intellectual and physical power to make smooth their operations, coupled with their client's political and economic power, their path cannot be blocked. They will manoeuvre their way even if it means eliminating one or two 'human impediments'. The missions remains clear, to either virtually or physically enter the target domain by all means. This was the case in Kenya. Later after the elections, IEBC could not allow access to their servers even through a court order from the Supreme Court, the apex court in the land. This research maintains that such defiance could only be possible if IEBC was not confident with content of its servers. The young and innocent KIEMS system had been molested and badly defiled. The internals could not be exposed to 'we people of Kenya' even if we were the natural parents of the information in the servers. The information has since remained a private part and property of IEBC.

Intrusions during Vote Tallying and Vote Result Transmission; the Raila 2017 Presidential Petition No. 1of 2018.

In his verifying affidavit filed during the Supreme Court hearing of presidential petition No. 1 of 2017, Raila Odinga reiterated the position that the Elections Act was amended to introduce Section 39(1C) that ought to have been complied with. The said section provides for simultaneous electronic transmission of results, from the polling stations to Constituency Tallying Centre (CTC) and to the National Tallying Centre (NTC) the moment vote counting at the polling station is concluded. It was Raila's contention that IEBC flouted the advice from Communication Authority of Kenya (CAK) to locally host its primary and disaster recovery sites and IEBC went ahead and engaged a foreign France company to host it. Raila stated that this defiance compromised the security of KIEMS exposing it to unlawful interference and manipulation of results by third parties rendering the 2017 presidential election a sham (The et al., 2017)

To entrench their intrusion allegations, the petitioners invoked the contents of the affidavits of Dr. Nyangasi Oduwor and Godfrey Osotsi. They claimed that on the 8th August, 2017, at around 5.07 p.m., barely 10 minutes after closure of the polling stations, IEBC started streaming in purported results of the presidential vote through the IEBC web portal and the media with constant percentages of 54% and 44% being maintained in favour of the 3rd respondent and the 1st petitioner respectively.[35]Dr. Otiende Amollo, counsel for the petitioners went on to show the court an algorithm formula that was allegedly used to manufacture the results and the will of the people. This formula which is said to have been developed by NASA's IT expert Dr. Edgar Otumba Ouko was; $Y=1.2045X + 183546$. Dr. Otiende Amollo elucidated that Y in the formula represented Uhuru Kenyatta's votes which were arrived at by multiplying X (Raila Odinga's votes) at any time with 1.2045 and adding 183, 546. According to the petitioners counsel, such prefigures therefore could only point towards one telling fact; that during the said elections, the purported results were not naturally or randomly streaming in from the different Constituency tallying centers. Instead, it was petitioner's case that the results were virtually being held somewhere and adjusted using the aforestated error adjustment formula to bring in a manufactured and misleading outcome as results. With the foregoing, the petitioners maintained that they had tabled sufficient evidence to tilt the scale of justice in their favour. They vehemently insisted that the electronic system of result transmission was intruded into by third

---

[35] Para 36 of Supreme Court Judgment on Presidential Petition No. 1 of 2017

parties who manipulated it and artistically manufactured numbers for transmission to the NTC.[36] And that any technology failure was premeditated, systemic and systematic.

Using Raila's disposition on the affidavit as a touchstone, counsel for the petitioners maintained that the delay and/or failure to electronically transmit the results in the specified forms meant that IEBC did not conduct the elections in a simple, accurate, verifiable, secure, accountable, and transparent manner in conformity with Article 81(e) (iv) and (v) of the Constitution (The et al., 2017). In the petitioners' view, all these violations of the law fundamentally compromised the elections outcome and the will of the people. The elections were neither credible nor free and fair. They reiterated that the Court had no choice but to annul it.

The petitioners counsel persistently and consistently poked holes on the concluded 2017 electoral process. They persuaded the court to believe that the entire process and the results were so inconsistent that they could not be relied upon to determine the will of the Kenyan voters. The respondents were pressed to the wall. The petitioners managed to convince the court that there was actual intrusion into the IEBC system. In response to the inconsistencies in the results, the IEBC counsel Mr. Nyamodi mesmerized the court when he confidently but unwittingly stated that the figures on the public portal and media were not results but statistics. Letting the court to speak for itself at paragraph 257 of the judgement, the court asked;

> "Where did the language of "statistics" as opposed to "results" emerge from? Was counsel disclosing the fact that fundamental changes had been made to the KIEMS system at the sole discretion of the 1st respondent without reference to all the players in the presidential election contest?"[37]

Mr. Ezra Chiloba, the IEBC C.E.O. while addressing the issues of the humongous number of rejected votes, he deposed in his affidavit that any variance between the actual number of rejected votes on Form 34C and the public portal were as a result of human error and did not affect significantly the outcome of the election.[38] In rundown, both respondents asserted that if in fact there existed any peccadillos as purported, the same were administrative, human, clerical, transcription, transposition, computation, data input, mathematical and erroneous recording errors which would not in any way affect the results.(The et al., 2017). To buttress this position, affidavits were filed of some presiding and returning officers who averred to having committed

---

[36] Para 29 *ibid*
[37] Para 257 of Supreme Court Judgment on Presidential Petition No. 1 of 2017
[38] Para 78 ibid

some minor administrative irregularities due to fatigue and inadvertence. Contrary to the petitioners claim, they maintained that the said irregularities were not pre-meditated and should be excused. [99]

Despite their great effort and skill, the court was not convinced. In the circumstance, the court could still not comprehend why the figures, which learned counsel Mr.Nyamodi referred to as mere "statistics" that did not go into the determination of the outcome of the results, differed.[39]The case for actual cyberspace intrusion was indirectly but explicitly made out. The court was persuaded and it believed. At least, above balance of probability but below reasonable doubt, that something was really wrong online and in the IEBC computer systems. This research infers that from the court's findings, intrusion during vote tallying and/ or vote result transmission in Kenya 2017 general election was real. The court found that the acts and omissions of IEBC during the electoral process were inexcusable contravention of Section 39(1C) of the Elections Act. It stated;

> "On our part, having considered the opposing positions, we are of the view that, the contentions by the 1st and 2nd respondents ignore two important factors. One, that elections are not only about numbers as many, surprisingly even prominent lawyers, would like the country to believe. Even in numbers, we used to be told in school that to arrive at a mathematical solution, there is always a computational path one has to take, as proof that the process indeed gives rise to the stated solution. Elections are not events but processes."[40]

Post-election Intrusions & Election Dispute Resolution

This research argues that post-elections cyberspace intrusion in Kenya was either to destroy evidence or to seek evidence of previous intrusions. At this level of dispute resolution, the interest was solely to win the case at all costs. The court was keen to serve justice. Petitioners claimed they wanted the truth, the truth which they believed was only available in the IEBC servers. The respondents maintained that the people of Kenya had spoken and that the voice of procedural technicalities should not be raised higher than the voice of the overwhelming number of votes. IEBC emphatically opposed the prayers for access to its servers. The learned counsel Mr. Paul Mwite raised information system security concerns. He maintained that such access would compromise the security of the data in those servers. However, after considering the

---

[39] Para 275 of Supreme Court Judgment on Presidential Petition No. 1 of 2017
[40] Para 224 *ibid*

application, the court overruled that opposition and partially granted the application. The court noted:

> "..we did not therefore accept IEBC's said claim of compromising the security of its servers, considering the fact that having spent billions of taxpayers' money IEBC should have set a robust backup system, nevertheless to assuage those fears, we granted the petitioners a "read only access" which included copying where the petitioners so wished."

What followed was a malicious, blatant and unprecedented defiance of a supreme court order by an 'independent' electoral commission purporting to be exercising authority on behalf of 'we' the people of Kenya. A report by the Court appointed ICT experts, Professor Joseph Sevilla and Professor Elijah Omwenga, who are holders of PhDs on IT and lecturers in Strathmore and Kabianga Universities respectively, manifested IEBC's disobedience to the rule of law. [41]

According to paragraph 278 of the supreme court judgement in Raila Odinga case (*Presidential Petition No. 1 of 2017*, n.d.), IEBC in disobedience of the supreme court order and in its endeavour to protect electoral cyberspace intruders at the cost of democracy and justice, it failed, refused and did not avail the following items either to the petitioners; the 3rd respondent or the Supreme Court; Firewalls without disclosure of the software version; Certified copies of the certificates of Penetration Tests conducted on the IEBC Election Technology System prior to and during the 2017 election pursuant to Regulation 10 of the Elections (Technology) Regulations 2017;Exact GPRS location of each KIEMS kit" used during the 2017 presidential election for the period between 5.8.2017 and 11.8.2017; and the list of APIs (Application Programming Interface) for exchange of data with partners. The Court appointed ICT Experts revealed that if IEBC would have given full information on APIs then it would have enabled determination of what manner of online activities may have taken place; other items not provided by IEBC were: log in trail of users and equipment into the IEBC servers, the log in trails of users and equipment into the KIEMS database Management systems and the administrative access log into the IEBC public portal between 5th August 2017 to the date of court order. In its conclusion, the Supreme Court disappointedly lamented;

> "The exercise was therefore a complete violation of the Court Order and the access was not useful to the parties or the Court….. It is clear from the above that IEBC in particular

---

[41] Para 277 Presidential Petition No. 1 of 2017

failed to allow access to two critical areas of their servers: its logs which would have proved or disproved the petitioners' claim of hacking into the system and altering the presidential election results and its servers with Forms 34A and 34B electronically transmitted from polling stations and CTCs." (*Presidential Petition No. 1 of 2017*, n.d.)[42]

Order of scrutiny presented a superb chance for the Electoral Body to table before the Supreme Court evidence to debunk the petitioners' claims. If IEBC had nothing to hide, then for its defence it would have without demur and in public interest provided access to its ICT logs and servers to refute the petitioners' claims. To the contrary, IEBC contumaciously disobeyed the Supreme Court order and in regards critical provisions. The court observed that the failure to satisfy a lawful demand leaves a Court with no choice but to draw an adverse inference against the party refusing to comply. The judgement reads;

> *"IEBC's contumacious disobedience of this Court's Order of 28th August, 2017 in critical areas leaves us with no option but to accept the petitioners' claims that either IEBC's IT system was infiltrated and compromised and the data therein interfered with or IEBC's officials themselves interfered with the data or simply refused to accept that it had bungled the whole transmission system and were unable to verify the data"[43].*

What followed the adverse inference was a historical directive, the court boldly without fear or favour ordered the 1st respondent (IEBC) to organize and conduct a fresh Presidential Election in stringent adherence to Constitution and the applicable election statutes within 60 days of the determination of 1st September 2017 as made under Article 140(3) of the Constitution. This research submits that the decision herein above, preceding cyberspace operations and the succeeding outcome of violence, deaths and economic hardship during Kenya's electoral period are classical impact of cyberspace intrusions to human rights.

In a nutshell, cyberspace intrusion events and allegations during the U.S. 2016 Presidential election, and Kenya's 2017 general elections indeed shows that cyberspace intrusions are eminent threat to free and fair elections, and free will. Accomplishing a genuine, democratic, free and fair electoral process is part of establishing a system of government that guarantees respect for human rights, the rule of law and the progress of democratic institutions (European Union, 2016). Bots are multipurpose, cheap to produce, and ever advancing. It's no doubt that

---

[42]para 278 & 279, ibid

[43] Paragraph 280, Para 36of Supreme Court Judgment onPresidential Petition No. 1 of 2017

unscrupulous and power hungry politicians and states will now deploy bots beyond ordinary commercial tasks. This research argues that political actors and governments worldwide have begun and will continue to increasingly engage social bots in acute political tasks; using them to manipulate public opinion, choke off debate, mud-cover serious political issues, vote preferred candidate or even to manipulate vote counts among other things. An action must be taken to protect democracy, to preserve human dignity and free will. It is time we entrench the human right to free fair election

CHAPTER FOUR

Having seen the argument on cyberspace intrusion as a threat to the right to free and fair elections as presented in the preceding chapters. This chapter will now give recommendation on how cyberspace can be made legally more effective in safeguarding the integrity of ballot and the will of the people.

Currently, three international spaces exits, are well recognized and widely appreciated. These are: Antarctica, outer space, and the high seas. However, this research argues that for effective regulation and operation, cyberspace should be treated as a fourth international space (Menthe, 1998). In prescribing recommendation for cyberspace regulation and accountability, this research argues that there can be no solution to cyberspace intrusions which is only specific state, or to a specific time like electioneering period and which solution ignores or excludes other states and times. This research argues, therefore, that cyberspace is no respecter or borders and seasons. In order to make cyberspace legally effective in safeguarding the integrity of ballot and the will of the people, cyberspace challenges must be considered holistically. Effective solutions can only be sort and prescribed; first, in general, by viewing cyberspace as an international domain, and lastly, by reducing and applying the general or the all-inclusive recommendations to a specific state or circumstance like election, espionage or even information theft.

In this chapter, the research argues that cyberspace can be made legally more effective in safeguarding the integrity of ballot and the will of the people by; having a commitment for cooperation among states; regulation via treaty law, domestication of such treaty laws, and by creating cyberspace awareness and education.

Cooperation Among States

In the recent past, cyberspace has become a major source of both tension among individuals and states. As evidenced in this research, cyberspace is a unique operating environment that challenges states and in multiple ways. These challenges include the cyber domain's reach, speed, anonymity, offense-domination, and complexity in regulation (Strength, 2015). This research argues that the issue of effective regulation and accountability at cyberspace is matter far beyond the efforts of a single state or group of individuals. Instead, it is matters calling for both bilateral and multilateral cooperation among states.

Cyberspace is a critical international space and in order to formulate agreed-upon norms for its operation as well as place its oversight in the hands of a broadly representative international structure, the cooperation must be free from accusations and malice (Swaine, n.d.).

Treaty law

There is no treaty provision that directly deal with cyberspace operations, this is could be due to inadequate State practice, paucity of official State legal views and lack of unanimity on norms (Banks, 2017). It is for that reason that it is challenging to positively conclude that any cyber-specific customary international law norm exists (Schmitt, 2013). However, this research casts-off any assertion that international law is mute on cyberspace, and the perception that cyberspace is a neoteric domain subject to international legal regulation only on a foundation of new treaty law. To the contrary, I incline to the school of thought that believes general principles of international law can be applied to cyberspace *mutatis mutandis*.

The Tallinn Manual 2.0

The general principles that can be applied at cyberspace with essential modification includes; state sovereignty, jurisdiction and State responsibility to cyber operations. One of the commendable attempts to modify these traditional international law principles to regulate cyberspace is articulated in a book "*Tallinn Manual 2.0 on the International Law Applicable to Cyber Operations*" this is a product of International Groups of accomplished international law scholars at the request of NATO Cooperative Cyber Defence Centre of Excellence(Schmitt, 2013). The Manual provides possible international law governing cyber activities occurring in peacetime. This research contends that the book provides a very comprehensive analysis of international law applicable to cyber operations[44]. It is, however, essential to understand that the Tallinn Manual 2.0 is neither an official document nor a convention, but instead, it is only the product of a group of independent experts acting solely in their personal capacity(Schmitt, 2013).

While adopting and endorsing some of the Rules and Comments in the Tallinn Manual 2.0 as will be outlined herein below, this research maintains that the book is trailblazing endeavour of

---

[44] ibid

39

world-class think tanks, and that it may serve as the first clearer road-map as we seek how cyberspace can be made legally more effective in safeguarding the integrity of ballot and the will of the people. But even for governments that are pursuing greater clarity regarding their rights and obligations in cyberspace(Manual et al., n.d.).

Rule 1 of the 2017 Tallinn Manual concurs that the principle of State sovereignty applies in cyberspace (Manual et al., n.d.). A well-accepted definition of sovereignty was set forth in the Island of Palmas arbitral award of 1928. It provides that:

> 'Sovereignty in the relations between States signifies independence. Independence in regard to a portion of the globe is the right to exercise therein, to the exclusion of any other State, the functions of a State(Ferreira-snyman, 2006)'.

The Tallinn experts goes further and classifies sovereignty into two prime categories; internal sovereignty under Rule 2 which provides that a state enjoys sovereign authority with regard to the cyber infrastructure, people, and cyber operations located within its territory, subject to the state's international legal obligations. The next category is found at Rule 3 and is known as external sovereignty. It provides that a State is free to conduct cyber activities in its international relations, subject to any contrary rule of international law binding on it[45]. The next is the principle of Due diligence. This is coined under Rule 6 to apply in cyberspace by stating as a general principle that a State must exercise due diligence in not allowing its territory, or cyberspace infrastructure under its governmental jurisdiction , to be used for cyber operations that affect the rights of, and result to serious adverse consequences for, other States[46].

As a general principle, the provision as to Jurisdiction is found in Rule 8 to 13 of the 2017 Tallinn manual. The rules states that; Subject to limitations set forth in international law, a State may exercise territorial and extraterritorial jurisdiction over cyber activities[47]. Rule 14 gives states responsibility on internationally wrongful cyber acts. The rule holds states accountable by providing that a state bears international responsibility for a cyber-related act that is attributable to the State and that constitutes a breach of an international legal obligation[48].

---

[45]Schmitt, M. N. (2017). TALLINN MANUAL 2.0 ON THE INTERNATIONAL LAW APPLICABLE TO CYBER OPERATIONS.(M. N. SCHMITT & L. VIHUL, Eds.). Cambridge: Cambridge University Press 2017. Retrieved from www.cambridge.org/9781107177222 10.1017/9781316822524
[46] ibid
[47] ibid
[48] ibid

It is worth noting that the International Group of Experts agreed that the customary international law of State responsibility undeniably extends to cyber activities. That body of law consists of secondary, as distinct from primary, rules of international law. Primary rules are those that set forth international law obligations. Breach of them results in State responsibility. Secondary rules lay out the general conditions for a State's responsibility, as well as the consequences of violating a primary rule[49]. Rule 18 advances the discussion on responsibility even further by providing for states responsibility in connection with cyber operations by other States[50]. The rule states that with respect to cyber operations, a State is responsible for: its aid or assistance to another State in the commission of an internationally wrongful act when the State provides the aid or assistance knowing of the circumstances of the internationally wrongful act and the act would be internationally wrongful if committed by it; the internationally wrongful act of another State it directs and controls if the direction and control is done with knowledge of the circumstances of the internationally wrongful act and the act would be internationally wrongful if committed by it; or for an internationally wrongful act it coerces another State to commit[51].

Rule 15 of the manual give provisions to the effect that cyber operations conducted by organs of a State, or by persons or entities empowered by domestic law to exercise any part of government authority, are attributable to that State[52]. Therefore, a State may not intervene, including by cyber means, in the internal or external affairs of another State. Prohibition of intervention is a norm of customary international law. However, this is the principle of non-intervention as coined at Rule 66 to have relevance with regards to cyber operations. This Rule addresses situations in which a State intervenes by cyber means in the internal or external affairs of another State, for example, by using cyber operations to remotely alter public perception, electronic ballots and thereby manipulate an election[53].

As a general principle Rule 28 encapsulates the principle of Reparation and states that a state must make full reparation for injury suffered by an injured State as the result of an internationally wrongful act committed by cyber means[54].

With the foregoing, this research argues that it time for states to consider a New Treaty to modify the Scope of Non-Intervention and Sovereignty and the countermeasure doctrines to make

---

[49] ibid
[50] ibid
[51] ibid
[52] ibid
[53] ibid
[54] ibid

cyberspace safer. This would require intense negotiations, and because information warfare has reportedly and largely been perpetrated by few states against many others, it is likely that many stakeholders will find themselves with unified interests in the content and the outcomes of such a negotiation("The Law of Cyber Interference in Elections," 2016).

Cyberspace Awareness and Education

It is a classical Biblical apothegm of great prophet Hosea that 'my people perish for lack of knowledge'. Knowledge is power and it the argument in this papers that cyberspace can be made legally more effective in safeguarding the integrity of ballot and the will of the people by disseminating knowledge via public awareness and education.

Cyberspace and its threats are here to stay. It would be improbable to think in terms of totally eliminating the threats and vulnerabilities. We must find ways to mitigate the intrusions, and this calls for organizational and individual cyberspace intrusions. States, organizations, academia, and general voters must be equipped with cyberspace threat and vulnerability information so they can keep themselves, their organizations, and their families safe and secure on the Internet. This is especially critical in areas including national security, electoral management, commerce and business(Mckee, 2010). At least, cyberspace awareness should upsurge knowledge of cyber threats, vulnerabilities, and solutions to minimize risks. This will help prevent states and electorates from making decisions and mistakes that could expose data, information, systems and networks to exploitation by cyber criminals(Mckee, 2010).

The lack of cyberspace awareness and education amongst adults and children negatively impacts their role of protecting their rights and freedoms. Awareness and education can be done through; workshops, seminars, posters, banners and even through national academic curriculum for pupils and students. It is clear that cyberspace security awareness must be shared responsibility; and everyone operating at the cyberspace has a role to play.

Countries such as United States of America, United Kingdom, Australia, and Canada have national cyber-security strategies; they all have at least one national sponsored cyber-security education and awareness initiative; and they are listed in the Organization for Economic Co-operation and Development (OECD) (Kortjan& Solms, 2014).

It is apparent that the environment in which the awareness-raising and education take place would be different for each target audience. But using the same example of voters, children and organisations; voters can be sensitized online, on radio and television shows; children can be reached in schools and homes; whereas organisations and state corporations or departments can be reached in the workplace. Hence, the environment should be taken into keen consideration when developing cyberspace-security awareness and education campaigns and programmes. This may influence the approach and tools to be used by the campaign or programmes (Kortjan & Solms, 2014).

The awareness can also take the form of voluntary service where volunteers are invited and are given training in several stages to help them understand what Cyberspace security would entail. They can also be provided with the logistics and content support during their own Cyberspace campaign or activities. Pupils, students and adults can become cyberspace ambassadors, form groups, associations, clubs and companies. For effective regulation, Cyberspace calls for a concerted effort from all actors.

BIBLIOGRAPHY

AL JAZEERA NEWS. (2018). US charges 13 Russians, 3 firms with election meddling. Retrieved from http://www.google.com/amp/www.aljazeera.com/amp/news/2018/02/charges-13-russians-3-firms-election-meddling-180216202400659.html

Albarazi, H. (2016). WikiLeaks' DNC Email Leak Reveals Off the Record Media Correspondence.

Bambara, J., Kapsis, J., Koonce, L., Ungar, R., & Webb, D. (2016). Election Law and Election Technology : What ' s New ; What ' s Next.

Banks, W. (2017). State Responsibility and Attribution of Cyber Intrusions After Tallinn 2 . 0, *53*, 52–53.

Barlow, J. P. (1996). *Declaration of Independence of Cyberspace.*

Beckwith, D. C. (n.d.). United States Presidential Election of 2016. Retrieved from https://www.britannica.com/topic/United-States-presidential-election-of-2016

Bronk, C. (2016). *Cyber Threat.*

Carlin P. John. (2016). Detect, Disrupt, Deter: A Whole-of-Government Approach to National Security Cyber Threats, 391–436.

Carter, E., & Farrell, D. M. (2009). Electoral Systems and Election Management, 1–34.

Clinton, H. (2017). *What Happened.* New York: Simon & Schuster.

43

Eichensehr, K. E. (2015). The Cyber-Law of Nations, *103:317*(November 2014), 318–379.

Enli, G. (2017). Twitter as arena for the authentic outsider: exploring the social media campaigns of Trump and Clinton in the 2016 US presidential election. *European Journal of Communication, 32*(1), 50–61. https://doi.org/10.1177/0267323116682802

European Union. (2016). *Compendium of International Standards for Elections* (Fourth). Brussels. https://doi.org/10.2770/923866

Faris, R., Roberts, H., Etling, B., Bourassa, N., Zuckerman, E., & Benkler, Y. (2017). *Partisanship, Propaganda, and Disinformation: Online Media and the 2016 U.S. Presidential Election* (Vol. 7641).

Ferreira-snyman, M. P. (2006). THE EVOLUTION OF STATE SOVEREIGNTY : A HISTORICAL OVERVIEW * Introduction The idea of absolute sovereignty is in many respects an outdated concept in. *Fundamina*, (at 10), 1–28.

Fidler, D. P. (2017). Transforming Election Cybersecurity Transforming Election Cybersecurity.

Forsyth, J., Liddle, R., Thomas, A., Moore, C., & Holland, T. (2018). How to Rig an Election, (march).

Fourkas, V. (1999). What is ' cyberspace '?, 1–3.

GCHQ and Cert-UK. (n.d.). Common Cyber Attacks : Reducing The Impact.

Gibson, W. (1984). *NEUROMANCER.*

Goodwin-Gill, G. S. (2006). *FREE AND FAIR ELECTIONS NEW EXPANDED EDITION.* Geneva: Inter-Parliamentary Union. Retrieved from http://www.ipu.org

Hitt, L., Ahluwalia, S., Caulfield, M., Davidson, L., Margaret, M., Diehl, A. I., & Windle, M. (2016). *The Business of Voting.*

ICCPR. (1966). ICCPR, (December 1966).

Introduction, A., & Communication, P. (2018). *a N I N Tr O D U C Tio N To Pol I Ti C a L C O M M Un Icatio N.* (J. Curran, Ed.) (Sixth Edit). New York: Routledge. Retrieved from www.routledge.com/cw/mcnair

Kalir, E., & Maxwell, E. E. (2002). *Rethinking Boundaries in Cyberspace.* Washington, DC.

Kollanyi, B., Howard, P. N., & Woolley, S. C. (2016). Bots and Automation over Twitter during the First U.S. Presidential Debate, (1), 1–4.

Kortjan, N., & Solms, R. Von. (2014). A conceptual framework for cyber-security awareness and education in SA. *South African Computer Journal*, *52*(52), 29–41. https://doi.org/10.18489/sacj.v52i0.201

Kostopoulos, G. (2018). *Cyberspace and Cybersecurity* (Second Edi).

Kura Yangu Sauti Yangu. (2017). The 2017 Kenyan Election: Pre-Election Statement.

Manual, T., Manual, T., Manual, A. T., Law, I., Law, P. I., Fellow, S., & Cooperative, N. (n.d.). *TALLINN MANUAL 2 . 0 ON THE INTERNATIONAL LAW APPLICABLE TO CYBER OPERATIONS*.

Maraga, J. D. K. (n.d.). Scrutiny in Electoral Disputes : A Kenyan Judicial Perspective, (277), 243–275.

Mckee, L. K. (2010). Increasing Cyberspace Awareness, (757), 1–6.

Menthe, D. C. (1998). Jurisdiction in Cyberspace : A Theory of International Spaces, *4*(1).

Miao Lu, & Jason Reeves. (2014). Types of Cyber Attacks.

Moynihan, D. P. (2004). Building Secure Elections : E-Voting , Security , and Systems Theory, *64*(5), 515–528.

Mugica, A. (2015). The case for election technology. *European View*, *14*(1), 111–119. https://doi.org/10.1007/s12290-015-0355-5

Ndulo, M., & Lulo, S. (2010). Free and Fair Elections , Violence and Conflict, *113*(2004).

Ongoya, Z. E., & Otieno, W. E. (2012). *HANDBOOK ON KENYA ' S ELECTORAL LAWS AND SYSTEM*. Nairobi: Electoral Institute for Sustainable Democracy in Africa (EISA).

Otieno-Odek, J. (n.d.). ELECTION TECHNOLOGY LAW AND THE CONCEPT OF " DID THE IRREGULARITY AFFECT THE RESULT OF THE ELECTIONS ? ."

Owuor, F. O. (2013). Election Management and Democracy, 14.

Polyakova, A., & Boyer, S. P. (2018a). THE FUTURE OF POLITICAL WARFARE : RUSSIA , THE WEST , AND THE COMING AGE OF GLOBAL DIGITAL COMPETITION, (March).

45

Polyakova, A., & Boyer, S. P. (2018b). The Future of Political Warfare: Russia, the West, and the Coming Age of Global Digital Competition the New Geopolitics. *Brookings - Robert Bosch Foundation*, (March). Retrieved from https://www.brookings.edu/wp-content/uploads/2018/03/the-future-of-political-warfare.pdf

Preiss, R. M. (2017). An Analysis of the 2017 Kenyan Election and its Potential Impact on Growth and Investor Confidence uncertainty in second.

Presidential Petition No. 1 of 2017.

Radcliffe, D. (2016). Ten ways the tech industry and the media helped create President Trump, (Silverman), 30–38.

Reynolds, A., Reilly, B., Ellis, A., Cheibub, J. A., & Cox, K. (2008). *Electoral System Design: The New International IDEA Handbook*. Stockholm: Trydells Tryckeri AB, Sweden ISBN:

RoGGKenya.org. (2017). ELECTIONS (GENERAL) REGULATIONS ,2017, (April), 1–44.

Schmitt, M. N. (2013). *TALLINN MANUAL ON THE INTERNATIONAL LAW APPLICABLE TO CYBER WARFARE.*

Shackelford, S., Schneier, B., Sulmeyer, M., Boustead, A., Buchanan, B., Herr, T., & Smith, J. M. (2017). Making Democracy Harder to Hack Making Democracy Harder to Hack Authors, *50*(3).

Shah, N. (2012). The Technosocial Subject : Cities , Cyborgs and Cyberspace, (March), 1–280.

Shea, J. (2016). How is NATO Meeting the Challenge of Cyberspace ?, (2), 19–29.

Strength, U. S. M. (2015). *2015 Index of 2015 Index of U . S . Military Strength.*

Swaine, M. D. (n.d.). Chinese Views on Cybersecurity in Foreign Relations.

The Carter Centre. (2018). *FINAL REPORT 2017.*

The, I. N., Court, S., Nairobi, A. T., Electoral, I., Electoral, I., & Party, I. REPUBLIC OF KENYA (2017).

The Law of Cyber Interference in Elections. (2016), 1–39.

Treverton, G. F., & Chen, A. R. (2017). Hybrid Threats : Russian Interference in the 2016 US Election, (November), 1–14.

Twitter Inc. (2018). *United States Senate Committee on the Judiciary, Subcommittee on Crime and Terrorism Update on Results of Retrospective Review ofRussian-Related Election Activity*. Retrieved from https://www.judiciary.senate.gov/imo/media/doc/Edgett Appendix to Responses.pdf

UDHR. (1948). UDHR.

Yard, M. (2010). *Direct Democracy :*

Zuley, C., James, C., & Cordell, M. (2003). A brief history of hacking ..., (november).